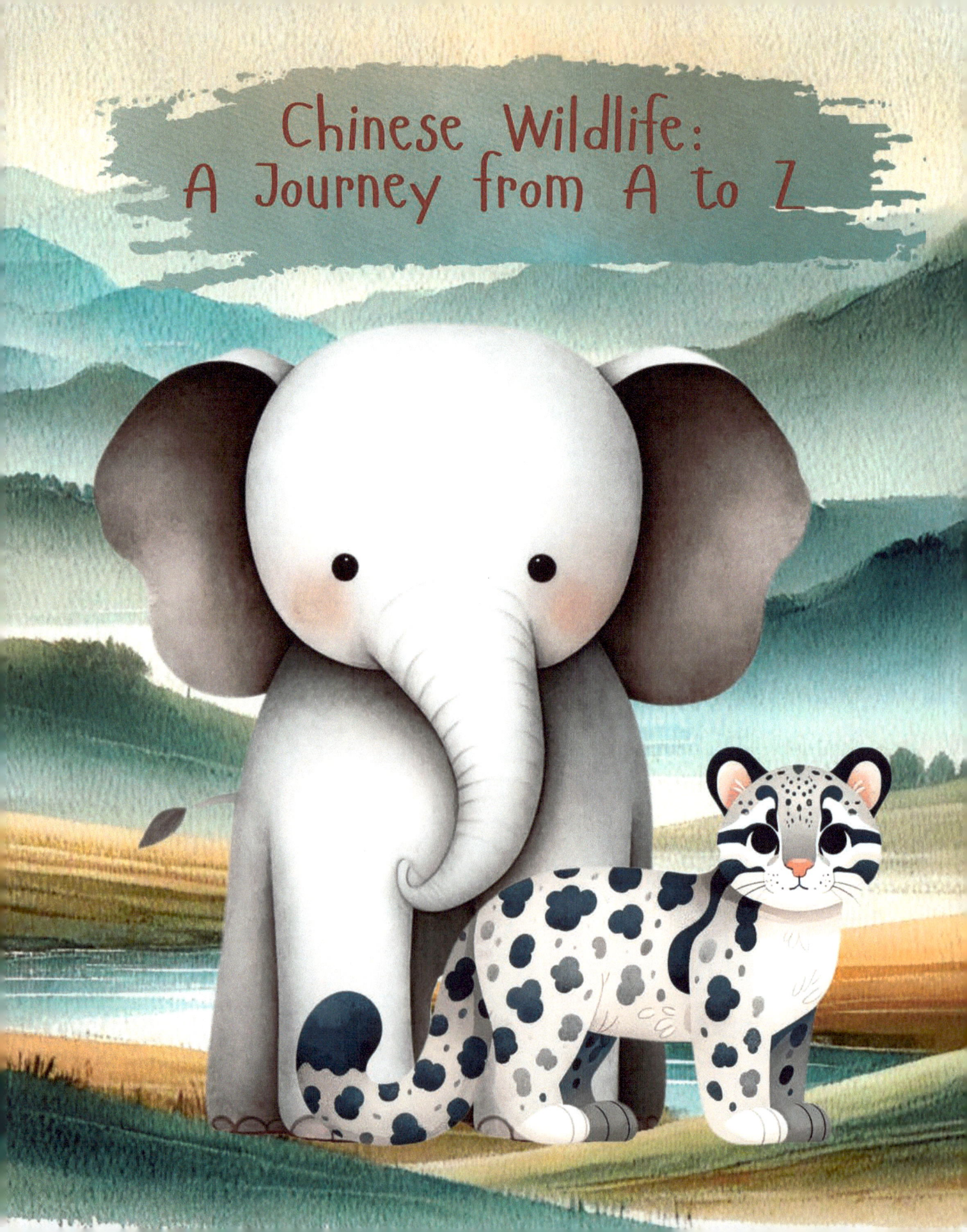

Chinese Wildlife: A Journey from A to Z
First published by FreemanJoyVentures
Copyright © FreemanJoyVentures
ISBN: 978-1-7638676-4-2

All rights reserved. No part of this publication may be reproduced, stored in a retrieval system, or transmitted in any form or by any means, electronic, mechanical, photocopying, recording, or otherwise, without the prior written permission of FreemanJoyVentures.

Batrian camel

Daurian hedgehog

Eurasian otter

Finless porpoise

Giant salamander

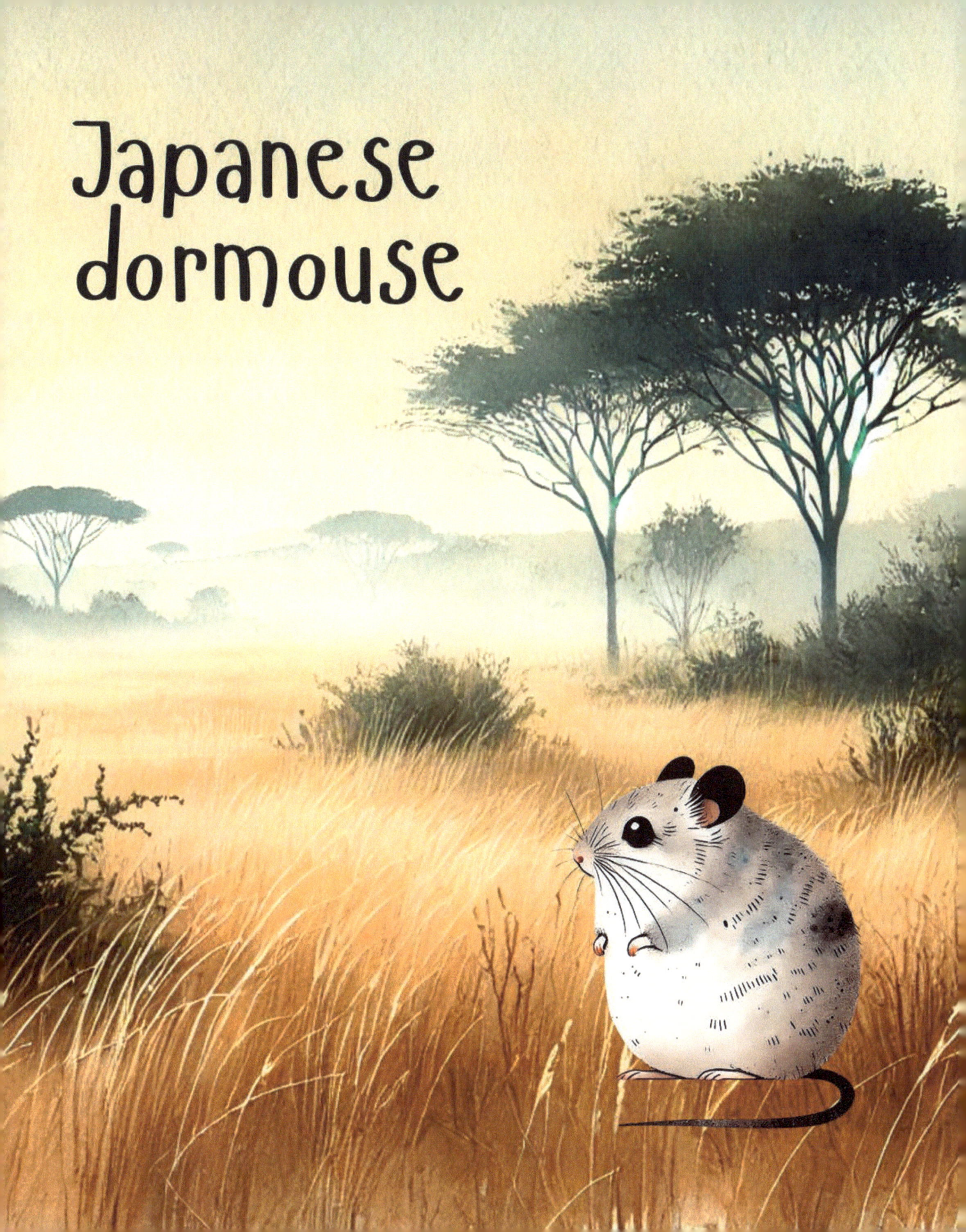

Koi fish

Koklass pheasant

Red-crowned crane

White-cheeked starling

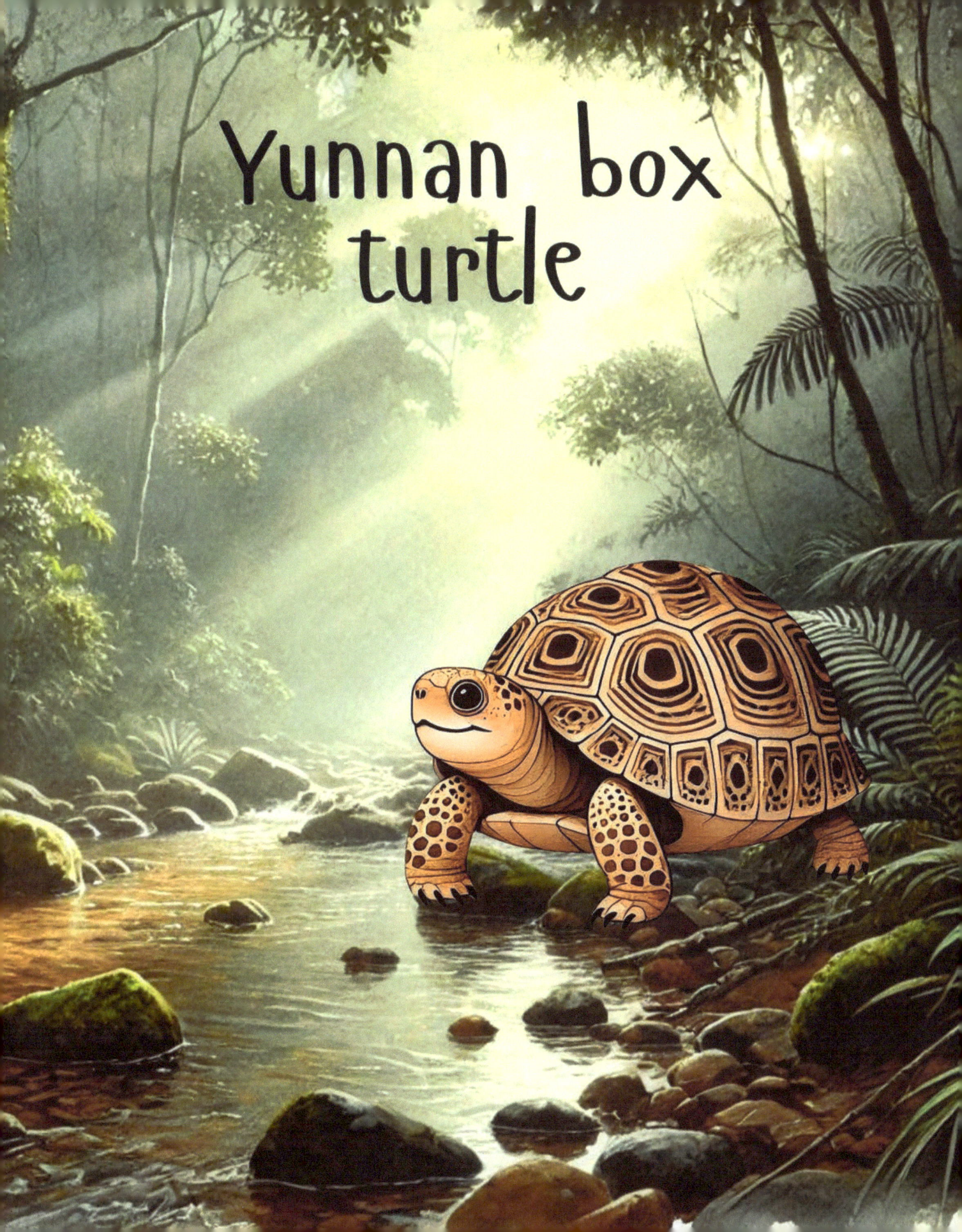
Yunnan box turtle

Zhokor